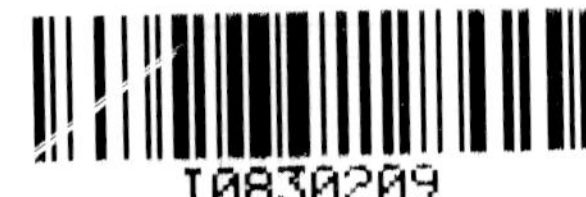


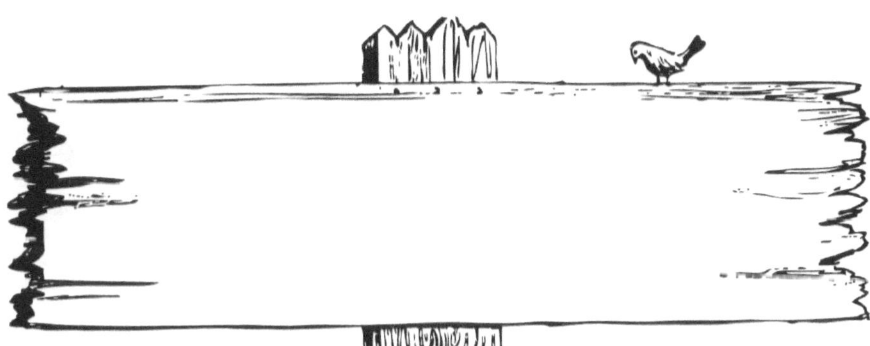

©2019 by WRITTEN NOTE - All rights reserved

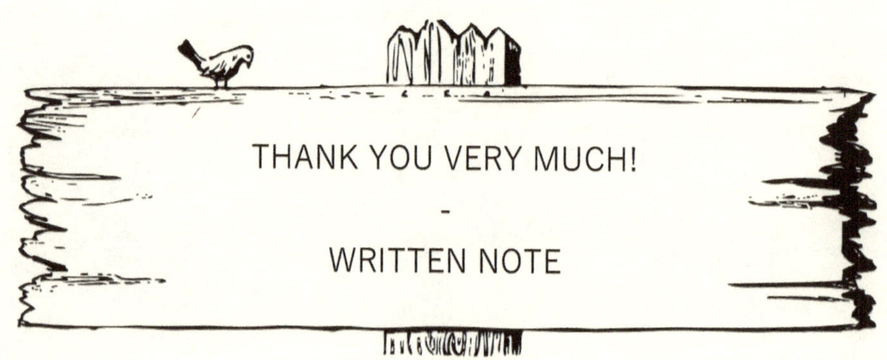


THANK YOU VERY MUCH!
-
WRITTEN NOTE

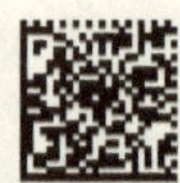
www.ingramcontent.com/pod-product-compliance
Lightning Source LLC
Chambersburg PA
CBHW031252250726
48655CB00005B/2189
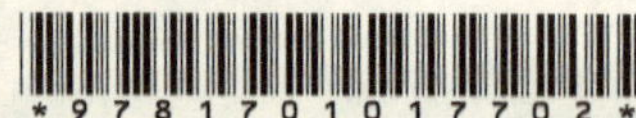